Sexual Intimacy that Works for Couples

I0558595

A Guide for Stunning Sexual Positions and Bedroom Pleasure Techniques for Strong Bonding in a Relationship

Grace Gary

INTRODUCTION

The bond between Gary and Grace was instant and cannot be denied when they first met in college. During their time together, they dreamed of a future that was full of love, laughter, and a profound and personal connection. Following the completion of their education, they tied the knot, firmly convinced that their love would triumph over any challenge that stood in their way.

Their honeymoon phase lasted for a much more extended period than the traditional newlywed period, and the early days of their marriage were filled with happiness. With a sense of both curiosity and excitement about what was to come, they were eager to investigate the sexual relationship that they shared. On the other hand, as time went on, fractures started to show in their foundation, which had previously been solid.

Grace began exhibiting symptoms of discomfort and avoiding sexual activity when it came to sexual encounters. Gary made an effort to comprehend and accept his wife's feelings in an effort to meet his wife's expectations and preserve the passion that they had previously experienced. Gary, meanwhile, had feelings of rejection and dissatisfaction as Grace's attitude toward sexual activity deteriorated. Their once-strong connection began to fade into the background.

With each passing day, the tension that existed inside their relationship became more and more apparent. The frequency of disagreements increased, communication grew more complex, and Gary and Grace both had a sense of disconnection and disorientation from one another. The revelation of Grace's long-standing problems with sexuality, which derive from previous traumatic experiences and the constraints of society, further complicated their relationship, which was already in a precarious state.

Grace was not able to triumph over her anxieties and inadequacies despite the steadfast love and support that she received from Gary. She felt as though she was unable to truly embrace her sexuality and share herself with her husband because she was unable to escape her past. Both Gary and Grace were devastated by the fact that their once-promising marriage had come to an end, and when the tension between them neared its breaking point, they took the agonizing decision to split.

The time that Gary and Grace spent apart allowed them to contemplate what had gone wrong and how they may have handled the problems that had caused them to become estranged from one another. In an effort to heal herself and preserve what remained of their relationship, Grace decided to seek therapy in order to confront the prior traumas she had experienced and the opposing views she held about sexuality.

How would you have handled the situation if you were in Grace's position? With the help of this book, you will become familiar with a variety of sexual positions and strategies that can assist couples in enjoying their communication and enjoyment in the bedroom.

Even in a society that reveres love as the highest form of human connection, the complexities of sexual intimacy are frequently veiled in secrecy and considered forbidden. The path that couples take to achieve sexual fulfillment can be a turbulent one, riddled with problems that put the very core of their relationship to the test. The book "Sexual Intimacy that Works for Couples" dives deeply into the complexities of sexual intimacy and provides a road map for couples to follow in order to navigate the often-muddy seas of their sexual relationship. It is through the lens of Gary and Grace, a couple whose once-romantic union is threatened by Grace's negative attitude towards sex, that this book explores the profound impact that sexual intimacy has on a relationship. Additionally, it offers practical guidance for couples who are looking to reignite the spark in their own lives.

This book challenges conventional views of sexual intimacy by drawing on real-life experiences and expert insights. It invites readers to examine the deeper layers of their desires, worries, and insecurities by presenting them with compelling arguments and examples. In addition to providing a straightforward examination of the hurdles that stand in the way of couples experiencing genuine sexual fulfillment, it also offers specific recommendations for overcoming these challenges.

The main point of "Sexual Intimacy that Works for Couples" is that it is a demonstration of the significance of communication, understanding, and empathy in the process of cultivating a sexual relationship that is both healthy and gratifying. It serves as a reminder that sexual intimacy is not only about the pleasure of the body but also about creating an emotional connection, trusting one another, and being vulnerable.

While reading the narrative of Gary and Grace, readers will discover a source of motivation and hope, knowing that regardless of how difficult their circumstances may be, there is always a way to achieve healing and growth. This book is a guiding light for couples who are navigating the complexity of sexual intimacy.

Few things are as intensely private, intimate, and enjoyable as having sex in the human experience. It's an essential part of our existence, yet it's frequently hidden, veiled in guilt, or ignored. Additionally, you will learn a careful and thorough introduction to a number of sex positions that can improve your sexual experience and strengthen your bond with your partner. It is a celebration of the joy, connection, and exploration that sex can provide.

Sex positions involve more than simply physical mechanics; they also involve mutual intimacy, creativity, and communication. They can lead you to new aspects of your enjoyment and a deeper comprehension of your partner's wishes. This book contains something for everyone, regardless of your goals—building intimacy with your spouse, exploring new sensations, or spicing up your sex life.

You will find a variety of sex positions on these pages, ranging from the tender and intimate to the passionate and intense. Every position is thoroughly explained and illustrated, complete with instructions on how to enter and exit the position, as well as ideas for customizations and ways to improve the experience. You will also find out how to make sure that your sexual experiences are safe, consensual, and pleasurable for both of you, as well as how to talk to your partner about your desires and boundaries.

It is a beautiful, natural, and incredibly human feeling to have sex. It's an adventure filled with pleasure, connection, and discovery. So, let's get out on this adventure and investigate the fascinating realm of sexual positions together.

Part 1

Understanding Sexual Intimacy between Couples

When it comes to human relationships, sexual intimacy is a complicated quality that covers not only physical but also emotional and psychological components. Not only does it involve physical contact, but it also involves the expression of love, trust, and vulnerability between lovers. It is essential for couples to fully comprehend the concept of sexual intimacy since it serves as the basis for a relationship that is both healthy and fulfilling. Intimacy in sexual relationships is fundamentally about connection. In this way, partners are able to communicate their feelings of love and desire for one another, so fostering a profound sense of intimacy and connection between them. The scope of this connection extends beyond the world of the physical act of sexual activity and encompasses the emotional and spiritual spheres as well.

Emotional Intimacy

When it comes to sexual intimacy, emotional closeness is a significant component. Being honest and vulnerable with your spouse, sharing your thoughts, feelings, and desires without the fear of being judged, is a necessary component of loving relationships. When two people are emotionally close to one another, they develop a sense of trust and security, which is needed for a sexual connection to be satisfying.

Psychological Intimacy

Within the realm of sexual intimacy, psychological closeness is also an essential component. Understanding your partner's wants, desires, and boundaries, as well as having the ability to communicate effectively about these things, is a necessary component of this practice. In order to achieve psychological closeness, it is essential to possess empathy and compassion, as well as the willingness to listen to and comprehend the viewpoint of one's partner.

The level of sexual intimacy is not fixed but instead develops with time. In order to sustain and improve it, both partners need to participate and communicate with one another actively. During the process of navigating the complexities of sexual intimacy, partners may face problems such as mismatched libidos, communication issues, or previous traumatic experiences when they are together. To ensure that sexual intimacy continues to be a positive and gratifying element of the relationship, it is vital to address these problems openly and honestly.

To have a complete understanding of sexual intimacy, one must be willing to investigate and find out what offers pleasure and happiness to both partners throughout the relationship. It requires being willing to try new things, expressing freely about desires and boundaries, and being willing to seek assistance if it is necessary. By gaining a grasp of the complexity of sexual intimacy, couples can strengthen their connection with one another and bring about a relationship that is emotionally and sexually rewarding.

The Common Misconceptions Regarding Sexual Intimacy

One of the most widespread misunderstandings regarding sexual intimacy is the notion that it should always be unplanned and effortless. Quite a few individuals are of the opinion that if they genuinely love their partner, then sexual desire and passion ought to come naturally to them. The fact of the matter is, however, that in order to keep a satisfying sexual connection, it is frequently necessary to make an effort, communicate with one another, and be open to experimenting with new things.

The idea that sexual closeness is solely about the pleasure of the body is another common misunderstanding. While it is undeniable that the experience of physical pleasure is a crucial component of sexual intimacy, it is not the sole relevant one. The quality of a couple's sexual relationship can be strongly influenced by many factors, including the degree of emotional connection, trust, and communication that exists between them.

Challenges in Sexual Intimacy

Communication is one of the most critical issues that arise in the context of sexual intimacy. When it comes to sexual desires, needs, and boundaries, many couples find it difficult to have open and honest conversations about these topics. Misunderstandings, irritation, and a lack of satisfaction in the relationship are all possible outcomes that can result from a lack of communication because of this. Mismatched libidos are another significant difficulty that people face. When one partner has a higher or lower sex desire than the other, it is pretty uncommon for the other partner to experience emotions of rejection or inadequacy. Understanding, being willing to compromise, and being able to discover innovative solutions that work for both partners are all necessary components in order to successfully manage these disparities in libido.

Prior traumatic events or unpleasant encounters can also complicate intimate partner relationships. Individuals may find it challenging to trust their partners and to feel at ease with them as a result of these experiences, which can create hurdles to intimacy. It is often necessary to seek professional assistance and to have a supportive partner who is prepared to listen and understand in order to address these traumatic experiences.

There are a number of external factors that can affect sexual intimacy, including stress, illness, and medicine. When it comes to maintaining a sexual relationship that is both healthy and rewarding, it is crucial for couples to be aware of these variables and to discover strategies to manage them properly.

It is essential for couples who want to improve their sexual closeness to have a comprehensive grasp of these myths and problems, as well as to address them personally. Through the cultivation of open communication, empathy, and a willingness to explore and grow together, couples can overcome these challenges and establish a relationship that is emotionally and sexually satisfying for both parties involved.

Part 2

Communication – A Tool to Enhance Sexual Intimacy

When it comes to having a sexual connection that is both healthy and happy, communication is essential. When it comes to a sexual connection, partners can ensure that they are on the same page by communicating their wishes, needs, and boundaries.

Communication also allows partners to express their preferences and choose their boundaries. When it comes to sexual intimacy, there are many different types of communication that we will discuss in this chapter. We will also discuss how communication can improve the overall quality of a couple's relationship. One of the most important aspects of sexual activity and intimacy is interaction with one's partner through communication. They may experience higher sexual comfort and happiness if they are open and honest with each other. It can be challenging for many people to be able to speak appropriately with their partners on sexual matters. A person may have a sense of uneasiness when they attempt to share their wants but are unclear on how to articulate them. This can be a problematic situation. In the following paragraphs, you will get information regarding many kinds of sexual communication tactics.

Efficacious communication

In order for communication to be made and for it to be effective, it is a thing that must appear.

Communication that is both effective and efficient is necessary for the maintenance of a healthy and robust relationship. It takes on an even greater level of significance when it comes to experiencing sexual closeness. Through communication, partners are able to convey their wants and requirements, discuss any problems or worries, and collaborate on finding solutions to any issues that may arise throughout the relationship. In addition, communication is an essential component in the process of establishing trust and closeness between partners. Couples who are able to communicate openly and honestly with one another about their emotions and desires are able to build a solid foundation of trust that enables them to explore and enjoy their sexual relationship fully.

Barriers to Effective Communication

When it comes to sexual intimacy, communication can be difficult for many couples despite the fact that it is so important. Fear of being judged or rejected is a common obstacle that comes up when people try to communicate. Partners may be reluctant to disclose their dreams or desires because they are afraid of how their spouse would react to them. The inability to comprehend one's own needs and boundaries is yet another obstacle that stands in the way of effective communication. It is difficult for many people to express what they want or need in their sexual relationship, which makes it challenging for them to communicate successfully with their partner.

Improvements in communication within a sexual relationship can be achieved through the application of a number of different tactics by couples. Establishing a secure and non-judgmental environment for communication is a crucial tactic that should be implemented. Without the fear of being judged or criticized, partners should be able to freely communicate their wants and needs without feeling uncomfortable.

Being open and honest with one another is another crucial tactic that should be utilized. Couples should make it a priority to communicate openly about their emotions, desires, and concerns, and they should also make an effort to listen to the perspective of their spouse carefully.

Additionally, it may be beneficial for couples to schedule a specific time to talk about their sexual relationship because it might be helpful. This may help guarantee that both partners are on the same page and that they are able to address any difficulties or concerns that may arise.

Part 3

Desire and Libido During Intimacy

Despite the fact that desire and libido are essential components of sexual intimacy, they can vary considerably from person to person and even within the context of couple relationships. We will discuss the intricacies of desire and libido in this chapter, as well as how these factors can affect sexual intimacy and the tactics that can be used to manage variances in desire patterns within a relationship.

Understanding of Libido and Desire

The term "desire" refers to the psychological component of sexual arousal, which includes thoughts, fantasies, and desires to engage in sexual activity. Libido, on the other hand, is the term used to describe the physical part of sexual arousal, which involves the response of the body to whatever sexual stimuli are present. In spite of the fact that desire and libido are frequently intertwined, they can exist independently of one another.

Sexual desire and libido are both susceptible to being influenced by a wide range of factors, such as hormones, stress, the dynamics of relationships, and previous experiences. It is not unusual for people to undergo shifts in their desire and libido throughout their lifetime, and these shifts can be influenced by a variety of circumstances, including those that are internal and those that are external.

A person's libido, often known as their sex drive or their desire to have sexual encounters, can vary significantly from one individual to the next. A person's tastes and the circumstances of their life also play a role in determining the outcome. There are a number of factors that might influence libido, including medical conditions, hormone levels, drugs, lifestyle choices, and relationship issues. At the same time, as there is no such thing as a "normal" level of libido, there is also no such thing as a "right" or "wrong" amount of libido. Some people have sexual encounters or the desire to have sexual encounters on a daily basis, while others may only have sexual encounters once a year or not at all. What you prefer and the conditions of your life are the two most important factors. At the beginning of their relationship, many new couples may engage in a significant amount of sexual activity, which will eventually wind down. A busy existence, on the other hand, can leave some people too exhausted or preoccupied ever to consider having sexual relations with another person. There is no need for you to seek the assistance of a professional unless you are experiencing concerns with your sexual urge or if it is causing issues between you and your spouse.

The Challenge of Low Libido
There are a number of other factors that can contribute to a decreased sex desire, in addition to medical disorders and the

adverse effects of some medications. These factors include the following:

- Performance anxiety, which can be caused by unpleasant sexual encounters or premature ejaculation, can cause a person to avoid sexual activity out of concern that it will occur again. The sense of being too exhausted to engage in sexual activity is a typical occurrence.

- It is possible that the obligations of work and family life will not allow enough time for closeness and sex due to a lack of time and privacy available.

- Over time, a couple's desire for sexual activity tends to decrease due to familiarity.

- Because of sexual incompatibility, a person's sexual drive may be affected if they consistently want more sex than their spouse or if they want a sort of sexual activity that their partner is not comfortable with.

- Sexual turnoffs — If your partner's physical appearance undergoes significant changes, such as gaining an excessive amount of weight, chances are that your sexual attraction to them will decrease.

- Depression is a mental health disease that can produce feelings of exhaustion, a lack of desire, feelings of sadness, and withdrawal from activities, including sexual activity.

- Excessive or insufficient levels of physical activity and exercise can have a negative impact on sexual desire and reaction. Researchers have shown that stress hormones might have this effect.
- When a person has been through a traumatic experience, such as sexual harassment, sexual abuse, or rape, it can affect their sexual desire. Physical activity might cause individuals to lose their desire to have sexual encounters.

It is possible that gaining an understanding of desire might be of great assistance in better comprehending our sexual desire. Two primary ways in which individuals can experience desire are referred to as spontaneous desire and responsive desire. For the most part, the kind of desire that is discussed and portrayed in romantic comedies and other forms of media is the spontaneous kind. Experience desire in expectation of pleasure is what people mean when they talk about spontaneous desire. For some reason, the sensation of desire seems to materialize out of thin air. You may be enjoying a cup of coffee while sitting at a cafe when, all of a sudden, a thought about sexual activity comes to your mind. Suddenly, you feel a strong desire to engage in sexual activity. According to estimates, approximately two-thirds of males and one-third of females experience desire in this manner. A different type of want is known as responsive desire, and it is triggered by pleasure. There is a connection between the sensation of pleasure and the subsequent sensations of desire. Noting that responsive desire does not mean that we should start having sex or engaging in sexual activities, even if we don't feel like it, with the expectation that sexual desire will then come up, is a crucial point to keep in mind. The act of putting in some conscious effort in order to establish a setting that is conducive to pleasure is an example of responsive desire. This may take the form of hugging your lover, simply lying in bed and having a conversation, or taking a bath with water bubbles. The circumstances that make it possible for you to experience pleasure will be entirely distinct from those that make it possible for another person to experience pleasure. When the correct circumstances are present, they might make room for the desire to take place. It is estimated that between 5 and 10 percent of males and between 20 and 60 percent of females experience desire in this manner. At various stages in our lives, it is not uncommon for us to experience a transition between experiencing spontaneous want and experiencing responsive desire. For instance, when we are in an exciting new relationship, we are more likely to experience spontaneous desire. This is in contrast to the more common occurrence of responsive desire, which is more likely to take place in a relationship that has been going on for a long time. It is normal and healthy to have both of these forms of desire.

Differences in desire.

Having different levels of desire and libido is one of the most typical obstacles that couples have while trying to achieve sexual closeness. The fact that one spouse may have a higher or lower sex drive than the other is not an unusual occurrence. This can result in emotions of frustration, rejection, or inadequacy for the partner.

The ability to understand, empathize, and communicate is necessary for successfully managing these disparities in desire. In order for partners to be successful in a relationship, it is essential for them to speak openly and honestly about their desires and needs and to listen to one another's positions actively. Partners need to work toward achieving a balance that is satisfactory for both of them, which may require them to make concessions and come up with inventive solutions.

Various approaches to the management of varying levels of desire

The management of differences in desire and libido can be accomplished through the employment of a number of different tactics by partners. One method is to arrange regular check-ins to discuss their sexual relationship and make sure that both partners feel heard and understood. This can be done by scheduling this strategy.

- Focusing on quality rather than quantity is yet another tactic that can be utilized. Couples can concentrate on making the most of the time they spend together, making sure that it is joyful and rewarding for both partners, rather than focusing on the frequency of sexual activity that they engage in.

- It might be beneficial for couples to investigate new methods to enhance their desire and libido. Some examples of these methods include engaging in new activities, fantasizing, or engaging in role-playing. Couples can improve their sexual relationship and strengthen their connection by being open to new experiences and discussing openly about their desires.

In addition, if we wish to increase our sexual desire, what are some ways that we might attain this goal?

- Reduce stressors: To begin, we can make an effort to reduce stressors in our lives wherever we are able to do so, despite the fact that this may be challenging due to the fact that stress is often an inherent part of life.

- Discover numerous methods of stress management: Although we are unable to eliminate stress completely, we can learn several methods of stress management. This may take the form of engaging in physical activity, meditating, discovering artistic outlets, or establishing connections with the significant individuals in our lives. Spend some time trying to discover what helps you to regulate your stress levels since finding what works for you is the most important thing.

- In order to figure out contexts, you should first spend some time asking yourself what kinds of situations in your life enable you to experience pleasure, and then you should try to create more of those kinds of situations.

- Connect: If you feel comfortable and supportive doing so, having some chats with your partner about what's going on for you is a great way to connect.

- Reduce the amount of pressure: It is essential to remind oneself that experiencing shifts in your sexual desire is very natural and can be considered acceptable. There is no indication that there is something wrong with you in this regard.

- Take advantage of support: If you have tried some of these things and still feel like you are having difficulty, you should take advantage of some expert support in order to receive extra assistance.

Part 4

Sexual Positions for Stunning Pleasure

Which of the sexual positions do you use during sexual section with your partner? Are you just new in marriage, or has it been years of marriage? Understanding and exploring different styles of position during intimacy can enhance the pleasure you get from sex. Although there are many various ways to enjoy each other's bodies, the missionary position is the most popular because it is so comfortable. Each of the positions pictured on the following pages may suggest a different position that you may move into. Certain positions allow for greater closeness through all-over body contact, the chance to hug and kiss, deeper penetration, and some that are challenging to maintain but evoke a sense of urgency and excitement. Whether intentional or accidental, daring couples will discover their variations: you might find yourself overcome with passion midway up the stairs or while conversing in the kitchen. It's crucial to follow all of your gut impulses and emotions while keeping a close eye on your partner's reactions.

Astride

With the man lying on his back on the bed, the woman can sit astride him and control the pace of their lovemaking. Facing him, she may squat on her haunches for a more powerful bouncing movement or, as here, kneel, supporting herself with her hands. This way, she is free to lean forward and kiss his mouth. From this position, it is easy for her to increase the intimacy by lying with her whole body along his. A variation is for her to face away from him, increasing the depth of penetration.

The astride sex position, sometimes referred to as the cowgirl or cowboy position, is a well-liked and adaptable posture that provides a unique fusion of pleasure, control, and intimacy for both parties. This posture allows for deep penetration and intimate eye contact, hence strengthening the emotional bond between couples as one partner straddles the other while facing them.

The ability to adjust the pace, depth, and angle of penetration gives the top partner a sense of empowerment and control over the interaction, allowing them to tailor it to their preferences. Additionally, this position makes it simple to stimulate the clitoris, which can increase pleasure and result in more powerful orgasms. Intimacy and connection are fostered by the astride position, which gives the person on the bottom a front-row seat to the activity and an up-close look at their partner's body and expressions. To enhance the sensual experience, this position permits hands-free exploration of their partner's body.

Leaning forward or backward to alter the angle of penetration or using motions like grinding or bouncing to change the sensation are some ways to modify the astride position. Since lovers may quickly change their movements to optimize pleasure and minimize discomfort, communication is essential in this position.

In general, both partners can have a variety of sensations and experiences during an intimate and adaptable astride sex position. The astride position is a fantastic alternative to consider if you want to improve your relationship with your spouse or spice up your sex life.

Crawl - An Animalistic Emotional Position

For this position, the woman is on all fours, and her lover is kneeling behind her; deep penetration can be accomplished. In addition to allowing the couple to push against one another, the guy may also caress his partner's clitoris, buttocks, and breasts in this position. This position, which is a rear entry, is perfect for when both parties want to make passionate love rather than gentle ones. An alternative would be for the woman to lean forward and brace herself on furniture while the other partner stands.

A wild and intense element to your sexual arsenal, the crawl sex position is an exciting and primal posture. This allows for deep penetration and an animalistic intensity as one partner enters from behind while the other is on all fours.

The crawl position can be highly stimulating for the partner on all fours since it puts them in a position of submission, which can lead to feelings of vulnerability and surrender. Along with providing for a variety of movements—from slow and seductive to quick and intense—this position also lets both couples experiment with their wants to see what works best.

The crawl position increases the feeling of pleasure and excitement for the penetrating partner by giving them control over the pace and depth of penetration. In addition to improving the overall experience, this position makes it simple to engage in manual or oral stimulation of the clitoris.

The crawl position can be modified by altering the height or positioning of the partner on all fours to change the angle of penetration. Other variations include adding bondage or role-playing to improve the experience. In order to create a fun and secure experience, couples should feel comfortable expressing their desires and boundaries, as is the case with any sexual position.

The crawl sex position is an exciting and daring posture that can intensify and heighten your sex experiences. The crawl position is a terrific alternative to think about whether you want to add some diversity to your sex life or explore your wild side.

Cross

In this position, the male lies diagonally across the lady as she rests on her back on the bed. He enters via her opened legs, and she gives a gentle rocking motion from side to side. She can exert pressure with her hands to control his motions. If the woman is in control and the male is lying beneath his back, it is simpler to keep the position.

A novel and private position that can enhance your sex encounters is the cross-sex position. In this posture, the lovers' bodies create a cross as they lay on their sides perpendicular to one another. The partner who has the vagina can regulate the angle and depth of penetration by adjusting the angle of their hips. Deep penetration and close touch are made possible in the cross position, which strengthens the bond and sense of closeness between couples. Additionally, it makes it simple to engage in other manual or oral stimulation, such as stimulating the clitoris, which increases enjoyment for both partners. Changing the angle at which the bodies penetrate to alter the depth and angle of penetration or adding extras like holding hands or keeping eye contact to heighten intimacy are examples of variations on the cross position. In order to create a fun and secure experience, couples should feel comfortable expressing their desires and boundaries, as is the case with any sexual position. The cross-sex position is a flexible and personal way to enhance your sex experiences and provide you with even more pleasure and connection. The cross position is a terrific alternative to think about if you want to try something different or spice up your sex life.

Cuissade

The name "crusade" for this posture comes from the French word cuisse, which means thigh. The man is on the woman's side while she lies on her back. He comes in from beneath her thigh, his nearest leg crossing her body as she lifts the leg closest to him and rests it on his torso. This "secretive" style of entering may contribute to the position's intimacy, as they are able to hug and kiss each other. It can be made more stimulating by the woman's ability to control her thigh to some extent.

The cuissade sex position, which is also referred to as the thigh tide, is a kind of missionary position in which the penetrating partner lifts their partner's leg and places it on their chest or shoulder. Partners may feel more intimate and connected in this position, which permits deeper penetration. Because their spouse is actively supporting and holding their leg during the cuissade position, the person being penetrated may feel cared for and supported. This can improve partners' feelings of trust and connection, making for a more fulfilling and intimate experience. Greater control over the depth and angle of penetration is possible for the penetrating partner in the cuissade position, which may result in more enjoyment for both parties. In addition to improving the overall experience, this position makes it simple to engage in manual or oral stimulation of the clitoris. Changing the angle of the leg to alter the penetration depth or adding extras like holding hands or keeping eye contact to heighten intimacy are some ways to modify the cuissade position. In order to create a fun and secure experience, partners should feel comfortable expressing their wishes and boundaries, just like they would in any other sexual position. In general, the cuissade sex position can enhance your sexual experiences by providing a new degree of intimacy and connection. It is a flexible and personal posture. The cuissade position is a terrific alternative to think about whether you're trying to branch out or spice up your sex life.

Cunnilingus

The art of cunnilingus involves using your tongue and mouth to make love to a vagina. If you can master this delicate art, every woman you learn to do it for will value you even more. It takes time, practice, and determination to get it correctly. The vulva is similar to the penis in that each one is unique and needs a unique touch to satisfy its owner. However, very few instruments can compare to the tongue in terms of the pleasure it may bring to a contented vagina. This article will presume that you have a basic understanding of vulva anatomy and are able to identify, roughly speaking, the mons veneris, labia majora, clitoral hood, clitoris, labia minora, urethra, vagina, and perineum.

How quickly can I go?

This is not a hostile act. Approach the clitoris differently than a firefighter would. The clitoris is considerably too sensitive for direct stimulation initially, rather frequently. Lick it, taste her, tease her innermost thoughts, and stimulate the hood. Listen to her and take your time. While some women scream, others do not. It will take some time to find out exactly what your partner wants from oral sex. Some women might want more stimulation, such as inserting one or two fingers into the vagina or possibly the anus. She might want your fingers to hold her labia apart so that your tongue can more directly access her vulva, or she might want your hands to reach up and play with her breasts. There are rumors that cunnilingus doesn't taste good. Ask her to wash first if the smell or taste offends you or causes you any concern. The majority of cunnilingus fans concur that a clean vagina is a good taste, albeit one that must be learned. A woman may desire more intense stimulation as her climax approaches. Fast, rhythmic stimulation works best in general to create a climax, but getting there shouldn't be rushed. Take your time, and you'll come to value what you have to offer her.

Fellatio

The lady in fellatio touches, licks, kisses, and sucks her partner's penis. Felatio is incredibly fulfilling for the male, but it may also provide the woman intense sensual pleasure when she feels his responses and complete abandonment of her. Fellatio: Speaking to a penis orally

Fellatio: What is it?

Fellatio, head shaking, blow-job-giving. Many men enjoy this type of stimulation, and many people—men and women alike—like providing it. The act of placing your lips on a man's penis in order to gratify him is known as fellatio. Other than practice, there aren't many suggestions for fellatio. The primary sources of stimulation are the lips and the tongue, so focus your attention there to help him feel comfortable. Pressure and rhythm elicit good responses in both men and women. A consistent, powerful stroke will be sufficient to produce the desired effect.

What happens if it tastes or smells bad?

Tell him to take a shower if you find the stench offensive! Even while your primary motivation for doing this is his enjoyment, you don't have to put up with his lousy hygiene! Furthermore, your mouth has millions more germs than a clean penis, if that worries you.

How does one "deep throat"?

The act of pushing the penis past your gag reflex is known as deep-throating. This specific sexual experience is really highly overrated. Giving fellatio still works best when done with the lips and tongue; take as little as possible to avoid gagging. For those who are interested, the fundamental lesson is still practiced. Then, close your eyes and focus, taking each quarter inch, assuring yourself that you won't choke, that you can take it out at any point, and slowly swallow it down. Take the penis as far as you can without gagging. Then, carefully get up off of it. Does the penis have any unique spots? Each penis is unique, with its sensitive areas and favored methods of handling. Pay attention to your partner. The best indicators that you're doing this correctly are the noises he makes and the way his body tenses.

Do I need to use my hands for this?

You are welcome to hold onto any part of the penis that won't fit in your mouth with your hands. Men like to enjoy as much stimulation as possible, and nothing may bring them closer to an orgasm than the sensation of a saliva-covered hand and a wet tongue.

69

According to some, the ideal posture for having oral sex is the "69 position," in which both partners place their heads next to each other's genitalia. This even makes sense for fellatio—the majority of penises curve upward, toward the head, and in a way that aligns with the throat's curve. It is challenging to enjoy and conduct oral sex at the exact moment, though. At least initially, focus on one task at a time. Try the position or kneel by his body. My sweetheart wants me to swallow.

The 69 sex position, sometimes referred to as just "69," is a position in which both lovers have simultaneous oral sex. Because it permits reciprocal enjoyment and a sense of equality in giving and receiving, this position is frequently perceived as intimate and thrilling. With one partner's head at the other's genitalia and vice versa, partners lie on their sides or top of one another in the 69 position. This enables partners to engage in simultaneous oral stimulation while varying the speed and force of their movements. The 69 position can also be adapted by placing couples on top of one another in a stacked position, which can enable deeper penetration during oral sex, or by having them lie on their sides facing each other, which can be more pleasant for more extended periods. In the 69 positions, couples should feel comfortable expressing their desires and boundaries; therefore, communication is essential. It's crucial to pay attention to your body's signals and your partner's, as some people may find this position uncomfortable or challenging to hold for extended periods.

The 69 position can be a thrilling and enjoyable addition to your sexual arsenal that promotes intimacy and mutual enjoyment.

Fireside

This comfortable position, which can be followed by cunnilingus, involves the lady sitting in an armchair with her legs and hands wrapped around the guy as he kneels in front of her. She can give herself more push if she leans back and rests his hands on the back of the chair. Particularly when you're near a fireplace, the fireside sex position is a warm and inviting way to enhance the sensuality and coziness of your sexual experiences. In this arrangement, one person faces away from the fire and comfortably perches in a chair or on a cushion next to it while the other partner straddles them. Sitting partners have excellent vision and easy access to their partner's body, especially the clitoris and breasts. Intimacy and closeness can be further enhanced by the sense of their partner's body rubbing against theirs. The fireside position gives the straddling partner control over the penetration's depth, angle, and pace, which can result in more intense and satisfying experiences. To enhance the whole experience, they can also excite themselves or examine their partner's body with their hands. Adjusting the straddling partner's body angle or adding extras like massage oils or candles to heighten the sensory experience are some variations of the fireside position. In order to create a fun and secure experience, couples should feel comfortable expressing their desires and boundaries, as is the case with any sexual position. Having sex by the fire is a warm and inviting position that can enhance the sensuality and coziness of your interactions, especially when done in a romantic atmosphere by the fireplace. The fireside position is a terrific alternative to think about, whether your goal is to have more intimate moments with your spouse or to spice up your sex life.

Futon

Try all of your furniture in this position to discover a piece that is the right height. Spreading her legs wide, the woman lies on the edge of a table, futon, or bed that is draped in cushions and quilts. To start, the man can bend down and give her a cunnilingus. He can then enter her while gripping her legs and supporting himself on his knees. He can regulate the angle of penetration rather well because of this. A version of the missionary position that makes use of a futon or other low, cushioned surface is called the futon sex position. In this configuration, one spouse reclines on the futon on their back while the other partner faces them while kneeling or standing at the futon's edge. The futon position provides a cozy and supporting surface for the partner who is lying down, which can increase pleasure and relaxation. In addition to improving the overall experience, this position makes it simple to engage in manual or oral stimulation of the clitoris. The futon position gives the partner more control over the angle and depth of penetration, whether they are standing or kneeling, which can make it more enjoyable for both of them.

Additionally, this posture allows for customization by allowing you to change the thrusting's pace and intensity. The futon position can be modified by adding pillows or cushions to support the body, changing the hip angle, or adding extras like bondage or role-playing to make the experience more enjoyable. As with any sexual position, the futon position requires open communication between couples in order to guarantee a safe and enjoyable session. Couples should feel comfortable expressing their desires and boundaries. The futon sex position is a cozy and adaptable way to enhance the intimacy and enjoyment of your intercourse. The futon position is a fantastic alternative to think about, whether you're trying to unwind and relax or mix things up with a new position.

Head to toe

The lady rests on her back with her legs extended over his, her toes pointed toward his head, and her head turned away from him. The guy is on his back with his legs wide and his penis inside her. It's the lady who is in charge. Sensation is focused on the genitalia since the couples are unable to see one another. One way to adopt this posture is for the lovers to sit on the bed facing one other with their legs intertwined. This variation on the classic 69 position, called the head-to-toe sex position or the 69 position with a twist, brings an additional layer of intimacy and intensity to oral sex. Both partners lie on their sides in this posture, facing each other's feet and keeping their heads close to each other's genitalia. The partner in the top position benefits from a particular angle for oral stimulation, making it simple to get to their partner's genitalia and enjoy oral pleasure for themselves. Because lovers are facing one other and are able to maintain eye contact, this position can help foster a feeling of intimacy and closeness. Since their body's angle and position alter how they experience pleasure, the partner on the bottom can experience oral stimulation in a different way when they are in the head-to-toe position. As partners sleep on their sides and support themselves with pillows or cushions, this posture can also be cozy and soothing. The head-to-toe posture can be varied by varying the body's angles to alter the oral stimulation's depth and angle or by adding further components like utilizing the hands to stimulate different erogenous zones. In order to create a fun and secure experience, couples should feel comfortable expressing their desires and boundaries, as is the case with any sexual position. The head-to-toe sex position is a playful and close version of the traditional 69 position that can elevate your sex experiences to a whole new level of pleasure and excitement. The head-to-toe position is a terrific alternative to think about, whether you're seeking to try something different or liven things up.

Lap

This is a sitting position that could be comfortable for lounging on the couch. The woman is facing him and straddling the man's lap as he sits. He can caress her breasts, she sets the pace, and they can kiss. She bounces up and down on him, using her arms around his neck and her knees on the sofa to support herself. She can keep her feet on the ground and, if needed, grab onto the back of the dining chair if they use one. They can get deeper penetration if she turns her back on him, and she could prop herself up on the furnishings in front of her. Sitting on the other person's lap with their back to them, the lap sex position is a straightforward yet sensual position. Intimate eye contact and close bodily contact are made possible in this posture, strengthening the bond between partners. This posture provides a sense of support and holding for the seated partner, which may be both reassuring and stimulating. They are able to discover the most enjoyable rhythm since they have control over the speed and force of their motions. The lap position allows the person on the other side of the other to see and feel their partner's body up close, which facilitates simple erogenous zone stimulation and a feeling of total immersion in the moment. The lap position can be changed by leaning back slightly to alter the angle of penetration or by adding motions like rocking or grinding to increase enjoyment. In this posture, communication is essential because partners can modify their movements to enhance enjoyment and minimize discomfort.

Having sex in the lap is a straightforward yet sensual position that can enhance your experiences with intimacy and intimacy. The lap position is a terrific alternative to think about, whether your goal is to enjoy a moment of intimacy with your lover or to liven things up.

Missionary

The missionary position is the most common position for making love since it is cozy, allows for a lot of physical touch, and has a decent penetration depth. The couple are able to hold and kiss each other simultaneously. Her partner rests on top of her, between her legs, while the woman is on her back, her legs open and her knees elevated. From here, the lady can stretch her legs apart as her partner spreads his, or she can move to clasp her legs behind his back or tightly close them underneath him.

One of the most traditional and private positions for vaginal or penis-in-vaginal sex is the missionary sex position. One partner rests on their back, and the other lies on top of them, facing them, in this posture. Intimate touch and deep penetration between couples are possible in this position. The missionary position provides a feeling of intimacy and closeness for the partner at the bottom since it makes it easy to keep eye contact and physical contact. In addition to improving enjoyment, this position makes it simple to engage in manual or oral stimulation of the clitoris or other parts of the body. The missionary position gives the partner at the top more control over the penetration's depth, angle, and velocity, which can make it more enjoyable for both partners.

Additionally, this position provides the ability to change the thrusting's rhythm and intensity, enabling a more personalized experience. The missionary position can be modified by elevating or spreading the legs to alter the angle of penetration, adding pillows or cushions for comfort or support, or enhancing the experience by adding extras like bondage or role-playing. In order to have a happy and safe experience, couples in the missionary position should feel comfortable expressing their wishes and boundaries, just as in any other sexual position. Having sex as a missionary is a traditional, private role that may be immensely fulfilling for both parties. The missionary role is a fantastic one to think about, whether your goal is to have a more passionate moment or to connect with your partner on a deeper level.

Side by Side

After engaging in mutual masturbation, it's simple to fall into this position, where the lovers are facing one other and lying side by side. This can serve as a setup for rolling over and placing either partner on top. To allow for deeper penetration, the woman, in this instance, has wrapped her leg around her partner's body and is pulling him in her direction while he thrusts. In this posture, the couples can make love while kissing and touching one other's genitalia.

Split level

This is one of several "split-level" positions that provide the partners with varying perspectives of one another and penetration angles. In this position, the lady lies on her back with her legs wrapped around her partner's waist as he bends. He has complete control and can use his fingers to stimulate her clitoris. With her legs dropped, he can either bring them to rest on his shoulders and lay on top of her in the missionary position, or he can bend forward and kiss her mouth, getting deeper penetration. A variation on the missionary position, the Split-Level sex position changes the angle of penetration to provide a unique experience for both participants. One person rests flat on their back in this posture, and the other person lies on their side, perpendicular to the first person's torso. To create a split-level effect, the couple on their side can then raise one leg and place it on the other partner's shoulder or chest. The split-level position enables deep penetration and allows the partner lying on their back to have intimate physical and eye contact. Depending on the anatomy of the partners, this posture may also stimulate the prostate or G-spot.

By modifying the position of their leg, the partner on their side can regulate the angle and depth of penetration in the split-level position. For both couples, this may result in more enjoyment and a more personalized encounter.

The split-level position can be modified by altering the leg's angle to alter the penetration's depth and angle or by adding motions like thrusting or rocking to increase enjoyment. In order to guarantee a happy and secure experience, partners in this situation should feel free to communicate their desires and boundaries. The split-level sex position is a flexible and personal way to enhance the enjoyment and excitement of your sex. The split-level position is an excellent choice to think about if you want to experiment with new sensations or liven up the bedroom.

Spoons

The two bodies fit so closely together that the position is called the "spoons" position. The male comes in from behind, and the partners lie on their sides. This is a comfortable and calming position, ideal for gradual, drowsy cuddling before falling asleep or when you wake up in the middle of the night. Later in pregnancy, when most other positions place too much pressure on the woman's tummy, it is also a comfortable position to assume. Intimate and cozy, the spoon sex position, sometimes referred to as spooning, involves both couples lying on their sides and facing the same direction, with the partner entering from behind. This posture is frequently linked to cuddling and can foster a deep feeling of closeness and bonding between lovers.

The spoon position can be both reassuring and stimulating for the partner in front since it gives them a sense of support and holding. In addition to improving enjoyment, this position makes it simple to engage in manual or oral stimulation of the clitoris or other parts of the body. The spoon position provides a close-up view and easy access to the partner's body for the partner behind, making it ideal for passionate kisses and caresses. Deep penetration is also possible in this position, and for maximum enjoyment, the angle and depth of penetration can be changed.

The upper leg of the spoon can be bent or raised to alter the angle of entrance, and it can also be positioned to increase pleasure by rocking or grinding. Since lovers may quickly change their movements to optimize pleasure and minimize discomfort, communication is essential in this position. In general, the spoon sex position is a cozy and private way to enhance the intimacy and closeness of your sex experiences. The spoon position is a terrific alternative to think about, whether you're trying to spice things up with a new position or to rest and unwind.

Spread-eagle

The woman lies face down with the male on top of her in this rear entry position. He bears his weight on his arms as she spreads her legs apart. Deeper penetration will be feasible if she lifts her butt off the bed a little, maybe with the help of a pillow under her hips. It is also possible for the male to roll into a "spoon" posture while lying entirely on his partner. A sensual and adaptable sex position that facilitates deep penetration and a feeling of openness and vulnerability is the spread eagle. This is a position where one party spreads their legs wide on the ground while the other lies between them, facing the partner's genitalia.

Spread eagle creates a feeling of vulnerability and exposure to the partner lying down, which can be pretty exciting. In addition to improving enjoyment, this position makes it simple to engage in manual or oral stimulation of the clitoris or other parts of the body. Since they can control the penetration's pace, depth, and angle, the partner at the top feels in charge and a dominant position while they are in the spread eagle position. Depending on the anatomy of the partners engaged, this position also makes it simple to stimulate the prostate or G-spot.

The spread eagle can be modified by adding bonds or shackles to heighten the sensation of vulnerability and surrender or by adding motions like grinding or rocking to heighten the enjoyment. In order to guarantee a happy and secure experience, partners in this situation should feel free to communicate their desires and boundaries.

The spread eagle sex position is a flexible and personal way to enhance the enjoyment and excitement of your sex. The spread eagle position is a fantastic alternative to think about whether you're trying to experiment with new sensations or liven things up in the bedroom.

Standing

They both stand, leaning on the wall for support. When the need to make love suddenly hits, this is the posture that's frequently adopted. The fact that moving in this posture is difficult adds to the excitement. Standing sex positions allow you to have sex while standing, which can spice up your sexual repertoire and add excitement. The following are a few common standing sex positions:

1. Standing Doggy Style: With one partner bending over and placing

their hands on a surface for support, the other partner stays standing. Deep penetration is possible in this position, which may also be quite arousing for both partners.

2. Against the Wall: In this position, one person supports themselves by leaning their back against a wall or other object, and the other partner encircles their waist with their legs. This is an excellent position for intimacy since it allows for face-to-face interaction.

3. Standing Missionary: With their legs wrapped around the standing partner's waist, one partner stands while the other lies on an elevated surface, like a table or counter. Intimate contact and deep penetration are possible in this position.

4. Standing Spooning: With one partner behind the other, both stand facing the same way. The receiving partner can slant forward a little bit for improved balance as the penetrating partner approaches from behind. Deep penetration is possible in this position, which can be incredibly intimate.

5. Lifted Legs: While standing, one partner raises the other partner's legs and either holds them up or rests them on their shoulders. Deep penetration is possible in this position, which may also be quite arousing for both partners. Though they could also call for some strength and balance, standing sex positions can be thrilling and daring. It's crucial to talk to your spouse, go slowly, and figure out what suits you both the most.

Standing Carry

With his lover cradled in his arms, the man stands. She encircles his waist with her legs and his shoulders with her arms. He can support her with his arms as she uses her strength to drag herself up and down to move against him. Sitting allows one to assume this position. It is highly demanding; however, it can be used in a tiny area. You can either resume sitting from this posture, or the male can gently drop his partner onto a table or bed so that the thrusting can continue there with less effort.

Swimming

With his legs extended wide, the guy sleeps on his back while his partner lies on top of him, placing her feet on his and her legs along his. There's a decent chance to make complete body contact and kiss. She presses herself up against him, setting the pace for their lovemaking. This is the most thrilling position for many women, and it's the most likely one to achieve an orgasm without direct clitoral stimulation. She can change the pose by asking him to close his legs, pulling hers tight while he is spread, or doing both at once. She can sit up facing him with ease from this position as well. Your sex experiences might become more exciting and varied by adopting the fun and adventurous swimming sex position. With one person positioned behind the other for penetration, both lovers float in a pool or other body of water in this posture.

The swimming position gives the partner in front a sense of freedom and weightlessness that might heighten their pleasure. To enhance the entire sensation, this posture also makes it simple to engage in manual or oral stimulation of the clitoris. The swimming position offers deep penetration and a novel sensation of movement for the partner behind. Additionally, this position gives you the chance to experiment with various penetration depths and angles, which will make you both feel more satisfied. Adjusting the body's angle to alter the depth and angle of penetration or adding motions like floating or kicking to increase enjoyment are some variations of the swimming position. In order to guarantee a happy and secure experience, partners in this situation should feel free to communicate their desires and boundaries.

You are having sex while swimming is an exciting and daring position that can spice up your sexual experiences. The swimming position is a terrific alternative to think about whether you want to try something new or just spice things up with your spouse.

Urgent

This is the perfect situation to find yourself in when the need to make love suddenly overwhelms you. If desired, all that is needed is to loosen your clothing. The man comes in from behind as the woman leans over the closest suitable piece of furniture. It allows both couples to push against one another and is terrific for quick, intense sex.

Part 5

How to find your Woman G-Spot?

Your partner will know what feels good more than anybody else, as is the case with practically all sex, so pay attention to what she has to say, especially when it comes to comfort and intensity. It should go without saying, so I won't overuse phrases like "within the comfort level of your partner" in this book. Urge her to speak with you, take a step back if it becomes too much, and adjust if anything else might make her feel better. Let's be honest: this document would not exist if not for helpful criticism. It goes without saying that every lady is unique and that you should consider what makes each person you are with feel good. While it hasn't worked perfectly for every individual I've dated, the approach I'll outline here has worked effectively for MOST of them. Being able to respond and communicate while maintaining your confidence is a crucial skill. Put this into practice. Regardless of the gender of the incentive partner— though if you close your eyes, it doesn't really matter—the advice in this document is still applicable. However, it is presumed that the receptive partner has female genitalia (except from the section on the prostate gland in "ON MEN"). Oh, and there's more. The majority of individuals in my immediate vicinity have reclaimed the term "cunt" and its negative connotations have vanished. In this document, I will freely utilize the phrase.

The Essential Steps

Cut your fingernails first. Put on latex gloves unless you and your partner are latex monogamous. Put cotton balls under your fingernails and cover them with latex gloves if you must have long fingernails for fashion purposes. Put a lot of water-based lubricant on your incentive hand regardless of how "wet" and aroused your partner is. Generally speaking, there are two basic patterns to using the first and second fingers of one's favored hand in the vagina. Throughout sex, switch back and forth between these two patterns as desired.

- Gently slide the fingers in as far as it is comfortable or practicable into the vagina, rotating them in even circles. It's essential to apply firm, consistent pressure to the vaginal walls along the entire length of the fingers at all times during the rotation. However, you can use a TINY bit more pressure toward the G-spot at 12 o'clock as long as you don't disrupt the rotational rhythm.

- If your spouse is on her back, position your fingers so that they are slightly behind the pubic bone and apply pressure upward. Direct G-spot stimulation works best when the fingers are moving delicately. You have the option of rocking back and forth or gently in a circular motion with your fingers pointed farther upward. Depending on the quantity and sensitivity of the tissue between the urethral sponge and the vaginal wall, hard pressure may occasionally be desired in this situation (see below). BUT WHY? This works so well because it switches between sensations of being **overly full** and **direct stimulation** of the G-spot. Thus, it's akin to having your head and fingers fucked by a massive cock. Additionally, it offers a fantastic and, as far as we are aware, ideal chance for G-spot orgasms.

Embellishment

You can expand your manual technique repertoire by including other methods. You can imitate fucking by thrusting your hand in and out. For added excitement, apply pressure upward as you withdraw to involve the G-spot. As you work over her cunt, you can stimulate the clitoris with your thumb—either the insertive hand's or another gloved hand's. Your non-insertive hand can be used for a multitude of tasks:

- Grabbing her hair.
- Holding her hands over her head.
- Having her suck your fingers.
- Holding her.
- Running your hands over her body
- Pinching her nipples, etc.

You can murmur passionate things in her ear while lying down or crouching with your head close to hers. Some people insert spherical, smooth beads into the fingertips of their gloves to enhance the sensations they get when they put their hand inside another person. Some people cut their gloves on both sides, fold them into a flap, and use their fingers to have oral sex on their lover's cunt while doing so (although if you plan to do that, you may want to get non-powdered gloves to make them taste better, or wipe the powder off YOUR side of the flap with a damp sponge). I am unable to fist someone because of the size of my hands vaginally. It's worth a try, though, if your hands are small enough to accomplish this with a female lover, and she seems interested. You construct a duck bill by bringing your thumb and fingers together while holding your hand palm up and your partner on her back. This can be massaged into the vagina by rubbing and even twisting the vagina. Once you pass the third knuckle, your fingers will begin to naturally and softly curve back to create a fist if your anatomy permits it. In any case, the entire process can take some time, but both men and women who are able to anally or vaginally take a whole fist report experiencing transcendent, spiritual states as a result. If anal fisting is your thing, check out Bert Herrman's _Trust: The Handballing Book_ for an explanation. And just in case I forget... If your partner is masturbating you as much as you are masturbating her, you and your partner may find that the techniques outlined in this document are more enjoyable (and remember, lubricant is important whether you're male or female!).

However, after going over a plethora of particular approaches, allow me to suggest that eventually, you can stop thinking about manual techniques altogether and be creative by letting things happen naturally.

Multiple Orgasms

The majority of women who have gone through both say that having several clitoral orgasms is more complex than having many G-spot orgasms. Therefore, don't let the fact that she is approaching you interfere too much with what you are doing while you have your hand in some luscious tart. Encourage her by whispering some words of support, and if necessary, turn up the heat a little bit. Otherwise, let her experience her orgasm afterward and into the next one. It makes no sense to set boundaries up front; instead, let her tell you when she can no longer handle it. Multiple G-spot orgasms frequently produce a pyramid effect whereby each one improves the feeling of the subsequent one and almost everything else sexual. However, whether the person of concern is you or your partner, it should be noted that having a significant ego/emotional investment in having orgasms, or several orgasms, isn't particularly sexually or psychologically desirable. Getting "goal-oriented" about something that's meant to be enjoyable is pointless.

About Chemical Improvement

And one more thing... Although I haven't done it in a while, I've discovered that when a female partner is high, the time between one G-spot orgasm and the next is reduced, thus leading one orgasm to flow into the other. One partner put it as "forgetting" that she had arrived. Thus, she returned very fast and, in a sense, incessantly. She once came in nonstop for two hours straight when we were together, and she was stoned (we checked the clock). I just wanted to let you know that it's possible, even though I'm not sure if this is a common occurrence.

Part 6

Analytical Notes on Female Ejaculation And The G-Spot's Presence

The anatomically defined G-spot is the region that lies below the urethral sponge. This might explain its function in female ejaculation, at least in part. It also clarifies why, despite the fact that female ejaculate has been demonstrated NOT to constitute urine, G-spot stimulation can make some women feel as though they must urinate when they actually don't. Should you wish to further your knowledge on this subject, you may want to see the movies _Sluts and Goddesses_ and _How to Female Ejaculate_. However, it should be noted that, even among those who find G-spot stimulation enjoyable, female ejaculation is not a common reaction to it; in fact, it is relatively uncommon. Therefore, every woman has a G-spot since every woman has a urethral sponge. The only things to consider are (#1) does she enjoys being stimulated and (#2) has someone applied enough pressure and the proper method to ensure that it IS being stimulated. In my opinion, polls that indicate a significant portion of women say they do not appreciate or notice G-spot stimulation are more likely to stem from concern #2 than from #1. Of course, that's just conjecture; I have no evidence to support that claim. Anyway, ask some of your friends to try what I'm explaining, and let me know what they think.

Facts about Sucking Your Partner's Cock for Pleasure

Fact 1

I don't know if it was because I was raised in a home with brothers or if I would have felt and done the same things if I had been raised alone, but I do know that I have been captivated by penises since I can remember. Now, let's discuss the "basic penis." In my opinion, oral sex is the purest way for two individuals to express their love for one another. With any luck, this information will assist you in removing any obstacles that might be standing in the way of your ability to show your male partner how much you care and get the same in return. First things come first. Observe the manhood. I do not mean a quick peek or a hasty, covert investigation. Give yourself enough time to persuade your partner that he will be in for a treat if he allows you to do anything you want with him, especially when it comes to his cock. In a well-lit room, lay him flat on his back on your bed. Hold his penis in your palm and observe it closely. It's unlikely that he will possess the willpower to remain gentle, but then again, you are honoring his very being. When it's evident that the person LOOKING at his cock is worshiping, few men can maintain their composure. His cock will get hard and in a position where your examination will have value when you first begin to touch him. Wouldn't it be wonderful if visiting the doctor for a checkup was just as fulfilling? For you to be able to identify the key areas—those that are responsive to stimulation from your lips and tongue—the cock has to be firm. Whether or whether he has had his circumcision will be the first thing you notice. Although not everyone practices circumcision, there are benefits and drawbacks to penises in both situations when it comes to giving your boyfriend the most satisfying oral caresses possible. Next, examine the penis's shaft in close detail. Near the outer end of the organ is a bulbous section that is sometimes referred to as the "head" since it has a slightly bigger diameter than the shaft. This is the glans penis, which is named after the Latin word glans, which means acorn. Take a good look at it; doesn't it look like an acorn? The corona is the outer rim of the glans penis. This connects the head and shaft. The penis's most delicate area is this one. When you are giving head, the majority of your attention will be focused on this ridge. To reach the bottom of the penis, trace this ridge around. As you are aware, I like to refer to it as the underbelly. I have a special affection for the underside! The intersection of the two ends of this asymmetrical circle will be clearly visible. The foreskin will also be joined at this location if your spouse is not circumcised. Tapping the tip of your tongue lightly on this little spot directly can bring your spouse to climax because it's undoubtedly the most sensitive spot on his entire body. Take your time stroking the glans and the vicinity around it. The penis shaft is located beneath the glans. To the exclusion of the glans penis itself, the shaft has few nerve endings and does not, however, stimulate a man to any great extent when touched manually or with the tongue.

The number of proven cocksuckers that think that sucking up and down on the shaft will get the guy off always astounds me. Folks, that's not it! If it works, it's because the back of your throat is tricking his glans penis. He's giving head to your throat!

The testicles (balls, jewels, whatever you want to call them, but let's not undervalue their importance) are located beneath the shaft. Since the testicles are so sensitive to pain, they are typically not thought to be stimulated sexually to any significant extent. False! If you give the balls the proper amount of attention, you can increase his level of pleasure! Let's return to the main focus of the issue now. The meatus is the aperture located at the tip of the glans penis. The burst of cum occurs here. I didn't want to sound too formal, but I could have indicated that semen is ejaculated. Other areas of a man's body react quickly to stimuli by the mouth.

Particular sensitivity is often seen in men around the nipples. My partner blasted me before I could even get close to his cock the first time I kissed his nipples. My spouse still gets really turned on by my lingual nipple caresses, even though I haven't been able to replicate this in a lab setting (he hates to go near the lab with me). Thus, GLANCE at your partner's phallus. Examine it. When you bend your loving head over his cock, be prepared to use your tongue and lips to apply your newly acquired understanding of his regions of exceptional sensitivity to his body. There's nothing you can do that will demonstrate your love for him more than to worship his cock!

Fact 2

The unfortunate truth is that the majority of people—men and women alike—have no clue how to suck cock. Most appear to believe that they are inherently skilled cocksuckers just by cunting their mouth, closing it on a man's penis, and bobbing their heads lustfully up and down until he climaxes. On the contrary! To suck a man's cock and give him the maximum amount of pleasure, consummate talent is needed. There wasn't really anyone I could ask for advice or counsel when I first started my search. Everything was hunt and kill. Suck and hunt. Discover the one tactic that would ignite a fire under him! I had to learn from my mistakes, and while I wouldn't want to stop you from enjoying the intrinsic joy that these events will provide, I would hate to see you lose a wonderful friend due to your incompetence and inexperience. Assume for the moment that you have used that chance to LOOK at his penis.

should examine every region of the penis to determine which areas are most sensitive. Because you now understand that not all components are created equal and have moved past the idea that all parts are the same. Try the following to see how your man responds and gather as much information as you can about his reactions: With one hand, cup his balls and lick the entire underside of his erect organ gently, using only your tongue, while his erect penis is pointing toward the ceiling. You will discover which parts of his underbelly he enjoys having your tongue contact most as you suck along them. Your spouse will give you clear indications as to which parts are the most enjoyable unless he is made of stone. Focus on these regions of increased pleasure as you find them. The area where the foreskin and the head's ring (corona) meet will be the most sensitive for most guys. Or were they joined before he was circumcised? You're going to create a geyser if you keep licking and touching this region with your tongue. I advise you to get him off this way if you're inexperienced and want to win him over quickly so you can experience the thrill and nature of his climax firsthand. As he prepares for the big moment, you'll notice that his penis changes. Every time he climaxes, these indicators will remain consistent, allowing you to appropriately plan for his cum. The cock's head can enlarge a little bit more than it does when he is erectioning normally. In an attempt to propel his body out of his cock with his cum, he can push his hips forward. And for the majority of guys, a clear drop or two of fluid will develop at the little, exquisite lips at the tip of the cock just before the cum. The moment of truth is near when you see this or feel the opening at the meatus through his condom. Full speed ahead, torpedo launchers! When you are sucking his cock, where should you be? On top of him, in a sixty-nine-degree posture, between his legs? Where? Kneeling between his legs and approaching his cock from the bottom, as opposed to the side or top, will allow you and your partner to experience the maximum level of sensation due to the structure of his penis as well as your mouth, lips, tongue, and teeth. Not convinced by me? Try out the different positions (I go over the methods to be utilized with each position in later chapters). Determine what suits you and your spouse the best.

Fact 3

Place his stiff cock inside your mouth but do not tighten your lips around the shaft. With your head, begin a circular motion. The cock will slide to different places in your mouth as you continue the circle motion. Watch your teeth on this one. A kneeling position will suffice, but it is also effective when your partner is on his back, and your head is directly over his cock. The circle should be executed in both clockwise and counterclockwise motions in a slow, purposeful manner. I found many guys in New York who seem to prefer this technique above all others. I met one guy who could circle a cock for hours, and I found myself having multiple orgasms while his mouth circled my cock. I didn't lose my hard-on after each cum. When the technique is performed correctly, it means many hours of unadulterated pleasure.

Fact 4

As your partner sits up straight, you get on your knees in front of him and lift his firm cock to expose his balls. Find the underside of his balls with your tongue. Now, suck him up to the very tip of his cock while he rests his balls on your moist tongue. Using your hands is acceptable when using this technique. This is a betting strategy that should be used repeatedly in succession, much like licking an ice cream cone or lollipops. I was raised in the South.

And regarding southern boys, one thing. Early on, we learn how to take it off fast when necessary. The one method in this book that very few men can stand doing for extended lengths of time without cumming is the lollipop lick.

Fact 5

Let's talk about what is arguably the most popular cocksucking method in existence right now. Don't bite into his manhood too profoundly. Later on, we shall discuss deep-throating. It's fantastic and not overrated, but if you want to become an expert at deep throat, you should start with the appropriate methods and work your way down. Sliding your moistened tongue over his head and closing your lips around the shaft at the place immediately behind the corona, take his cock in your mouth. Don't just part your lips to reveal his cock. Insert it using a slide. He'll find it far more enjoyable. Put your hand around his penis shaft. Keep in mind that the shaft is not very responsive to any form of stimulation. You can give him the impression that his penis is encased by putting your hand over it. You now have a few choices. Make sure your moist lips remain in contact with the coronal ridge while you try to spin your head from side to side. Move your hand softly up and down the shaft as you work. He might try to shove your head down the shaft of his penis when he climaxes. He desires to cover you with his cock. If you deep throat at this stage when you are learning his climax, you will miss the subtleties. Instead, once he reaches his climax, softly suck around the corona to heighten his pleasure and orgasm's force. With further practice, you'll be able to sense when he's about to reach his climax and be primed for that first spurt out of the rubber.

Fact 6

This fundamental method can be improved one more time to increase the intensity of his orgasm. Even though he is spasming and ejaculating as a reflex, the semen cannot escape if you place your thumb at the base of the penis in a way that blocks the tube through which the semen erupts. You can hold off on getting his cum for a few extended moments if you suck hard on the head of his cock at the same time. It will continue much longer and be just as strong when you eventually let the cum burst. You'll be shocked by the power of his cum, even though you just postpone it for a brief period. These methods form the foundation of cocksucking. Don't go past these until you have mastered not only the techniques but also the ability to read and analyze your partner's reactions to the point where you understand exactly how he is responding to what you are doing. You are prepared for the subtler, more sophisticated tactics after you have achieved this stage. Don't let your slavishness prevent you from enjoying the joy of self-discovery. Make your cocksucking as unique as your signature by figuring out what suits you and your partner. You want your boyfriend to recognize you among a hundred slobbering cocksuckers, after all.

Fact 7

A gag reflex was among the first things you experienced when you started sucking cock. The majority of men appear to want to shove their cocks down your mouth as far as possible. Especially right now while they're cum! For a brief period, consider that the average length of a Caucasian cock is five to five and a half inches, whereas the average size of your oral cavity is three to three and a half inches. It would seem that putting all that cock in your mouth is impossible due to natural principles. It is feasible. You likely know someone who can accomplish it, which is why you initially bought this book. It is feasible to become proficient in the required method. Not to be dull, but you will start to comprehend the conditions that let you take his hard cock down your throat and into your mouth if you know a little bit about your anatomy. The fact that your tongue has an approximately 90-degree curve that leads down into your throat is the most significant barrier to taking all of his cock into your throat. Hence, getting the cock past that angle should be your initial priority. Get beyond the dangle's angle! Get into a position where you can turn your head so that your mouth and throat nearly lie in a straight line to practice this. To do this, it is ideal to lie on a bed with your body stretched out across it and your head tilted severely back, with your head close to the edge. This will allow your lover to approach you so that his cock can be inserted so profoundly that it presses on your lips. It will also put your mouth and throat almost in a line.

Fact 8

Today, we will work on developing the bodily reaction that needs to be reduced in order to appreciate the art of deep penetration properly. The body's innate inclination to gag in response to alien objects, such as a profoundly thrusting cock shoved down your throat. This propensity can be avoided by fully relaxing your throat at the precise moment of entry. Maintaining this state of calm throughout the deep-throating is equally vital. As you figure out the most comfortable course of action, let him shove his penis down your throat and hold it there. You can't move or provide him with any more stimulation than just keeping your mouth shut tight around his pulsating cock because of your position. Try using your tongue to massage his underbelly if you can! Only after you fully push your lover can you unwind and take his cock in this manner. Your spouse has complete authority. He has to start the motion and keep it going. This is the only exercise where you give your partner complete control over the circumstance. For the first time, he can push his cock as far into your throat as he pleases, which is why he will love this. Your companion is now doing an in-and-out motion similar to fucking. He ought to begin cautiously, mainly if this is the two of you's first time doing this. After all, he denies himself one of life's greatest joys if he injures you. There is no room for him to modify the motion from side to side. Therefore his only additional need for this oral exercise is to keep the motion in the same direction the entire time. Another word of warning. When your lover first begins to cum, don't allow him to get carried away. The most crucial takeaway from this practice is that he will be able to push his cock all the way inside your oral canal for the first time at that unique moment! His only additional instruction for the workout is to maintain the same motion across your lips while he cums. You won't have to worry about swallowing his cum due to your position in bed. Not only does he have a condom on his dick, though. He has gotten his cock BEYOND your gag reflex, which is the reason! His sperm would shoot straight into your stomach if there were no rubber! Neither of you will suffer harm or discomfort if you and your partner are aware of what it is you are attempting to accomplish and the potential issues that could "cum" up along the way. While it is likely that some people will never learn to use the "deep throat" technique, this does not lessen your status as a cocksucker. When your lover is pushing his cock all the way down your throat, you have to let go of every tension in your throat. It isn't easy to do this for your spouse to get it off totally, and it might take more practice than today. It's possible that even though you can take your partner all the way down your throat, you won't be able to keep your throat relaxed until he lets loose. It's my genuine hope that your partner will see that this isn't a rejection of him or what he's offering you and that you don't stop here and believe you'll never be able to perfect the "deep throat" technique. Keep practicing this lesson. I know many couples who have focused solely on this lesson for ten months. You will be able to take his cock deeper and longer down your throat with each practice session, so keep up the excellent work. In the end, you'll be successful. You'll ace this one if you have the motivation!

Fact 9

Let's now discuss the family jewels, another essential part of your partner's anatomy that shouldn't be disregarded. There are two items more than any other that can make your partner feel better. The balls are not typically thought of as the primary sexual object by many individuals. Like in lesson eight, a certain level of confidence must be established between the two of you before he will voluntarily provide you unrestricted use of these two delightful pearls because many guys are susceptible! Start today's lesson by giving his balls a light tongue lick. You might start playing with your partner's nipples with your fingers as he grows more trusting, gently increasing or lowering the intensity as you see how he reacts. While you are bathing his balls with your tongue, you might want to give him a little pat on the cock with your hand. Just as you have the right to put restrictions on the back of your neck until you are totally ready to welcome him, keep in mind that the balls are incredibly sensitive to pain and that if you do not respect any limits he places on them, he will lose trust in you. Once you have established this level of confidence, you can suck both of his balls in your mouth. If you thoroughly wet them with your tongue before putting them in your mouth, he will be more responsive to this. Your spouse will have microscopic hairs on his testicles unless he's into the latest craze of shaving his entire body. You won't unintentionally create pain by pulling on the balls because you will have pressed these hairs down along the sac's surface by giving them a thorough tongue massage before putting them in your mouth. This may seem like a little lesson, but when you take the time to get to know your partner's testicles, you will uncover a whole new universe of feelings!

Fact 10

Although I was hesitant to put this in your lesson plan, I ultimately concluded that my obligation to provide you with the resources to be the best cocksucker you can be will be fulfilled if you are aware of the safest manner to do this technique. Analingus. Your tongue is inserted into his anal orifice. You are sucking your ass. Make sure your companion is clean before you even contemplate doing this, straight from the shower. Over the butt, place a piece of Saran wrap. You should never let your tongue touch the actual anal surface. Your partner should be lying on his back with his legs extended and his knees near his shoulders for this instruction. This gives you access to his butthole and spreads his buttocks apart. You most likely believe that in order for your partner to enjoy this approach fully, genuine penetration of the asshole itself is required. Not so enchanted! Because the nerve endings surrounding the anus are non-discriminating, licking the area as though you were sticking your tongue up his butt will get him just as thoroughly and effectively! This method alone, as with some of your other courses, won't usually get him to cum, but in my opinion, it's crucial to be aware of every part of your partner's body to provide him with the most possible pleasure. After many hours of enjoyment, you might discover that you need to focus on other things to offer him the fulfillment he deserves. Due to its potent stimulant properties, analingus can produce a strong and quick cum when paired with additional actions like aggressive hand stimulation on his cock!

Fact 11

All you need for the majority of our lessons is a condom, your partner, and yourself. Perhaps some Saran wrap. A pair of plastic gloves. A mini-vibrator is yet another item that will increase your enjoyment. You might wish to start using your finger for this lesson. Then, as the two of you get to know one another better, you notice that your spouse begins to show some interest in the vibrator and its potential benefits. Start a gentle, lighthearted search about his ass as you are paying him attention. It will intensify the sensations that your lips, tongue, and throat are providing his cock to feel a finger toying with his butt because many guys are susceptible in this area. Put your gloved finger gently in his butt as soon as he relaxes and gives you access. Investigate the velvety feelings on the edges of his opening gradually. You will be in the prostate gland region once your finger is entirely within his asshole. Your companion will feel some of the most amazing feelings as you massage this gland with your finger.

The first time I experienced this feeling, I went to the doctor for a physical examination. I was eager to get home so my partner could try it out on me one more. I wanted to feel the sensations that the doctor unintentionally created again and again, even though it was a little awkward to cum in the doctor's office! For this lesson, essentially, all you need is a gloved finger. But according to some Cocksuckers Club of America members, a mini-vibrator is a fantastic tool for this kind of stimulation. The feelings against the prostate gland are intensified even further by the vibrations it generates, and it is about the same length as a typical finger! You will next need to find out which way your spouse prefers if he likes this stimulation. While some men do not mind, others enjoy an in-and-out motion with the finger or vibrator. This hurts me personally because it feels too much like a stab in the dark. My preference is to press the finger or vibrator up against the prostate gland and let it work as hard as it can. You ought to employ your partner's preferred strategy. One more thing. Your lover will naturally want to get the finger or vibrator out of his asshole when you cums. Anything that gets in the path will be driven out when the asshole muscles spasm. But you have to stop this if you want to maximize his pleasure.

To maximize the stimulation of sperm production, firmly hold your finger or the vibrator in place. I've fielded a lot of questions regarding the vibrators that surround the cock. Does it enhance the feeling or not? For my partner, it works, but not for me. That appears to be the consensus among FRENCH CUISINE MAGAZINE readers as well. Try the vibrator around the penis as long as you have it handy, in my opinion. As you are licking his private parts. as you're sucking his behind. Feel free to use the vibrator around his balls and dick if he gets into it. Don't try it again, of course, if he detests the sensation.

Fact 12

There will be moments when you'll want to let him go quickly! I always advise Southern lads to start with this one and work their way up to more. However, I purposely waited until now to offer this technique because I was hoping you could become an expert in all facets of oral lovemaking. You've evolved into a more complete cocksucker since lesson four. If he finds out that this isn't the only ruse you're doing on him, he'll appreciate it even more! It's a straightforward technique to pick up if you know the fundamentals of your partner's cock anatomy. Put your lips on your partner's cock and slowly spin your moist lips around the coronal ridge located at the rear of his penis. This works since your partner's cock's most sensitive place is here, and it doesn't take any advanced cocksucking technique. You don't have to be an expert cocksucker. Finding the most sensitive region surrounding the coronal area is all that is required. You can get a robust and rapid cum by constantly sucking on this part of his cock. To get him off, you don't have to bob your head up and down on his cock. Getting him hard again after he cums is another way to apply this method, and you'll soon find him rippling, eager to go again.

Fact 13

If you find yourself revisiting this lesson for a second time, don't be alarmed. At the conclusion of lesson 12, we had a little conversation about how to get him going again if he had recently cum. Now that you have your man off your back let's focus on some strategies to get him back on. To keep him hard, not only to make him hard. Enough to make you want to cum again! You might need to use other strategies after he has cum to keep him engaged and challenging. Even if that's not the case for all guys, a sizable percentage of us grow tired after just one climax, and even though you can make your spouse cum again, it will take some time. Usually, cocksucking by yourself at this point won't get him off. To get the juices flowing for a second and third time, you'll need to mix some of the earlier techniques you learned with your fundamental cocksucking technique. Now is the moment to explore his body without hesitation.

His balls, his asshole, his nipples. His underarms. The lobes of his ears. You can really go into his body and explore all those sexual parts that you overlooked when you were only focused on his cock during the second cum. His navel. His toenails. The lack of pressure to force him to climax in a set amount of time is one of the most exciting aspects of the second cum, in my opinion. You have an endless amount of time to immerse your entire body in a tongue bath thoroughly. You can safely and thoroughly examine his physique to truly get to know it all, including his incredible dick! This is simply an indication that you are becoming a serious cock-flesh aficionado. A title I'm happy to   have.

Fact 14

Sixty-Nine: Sometimes, giving your spouse oral enjoyment isn't the best course of action. Unintentionally, one of you will "let up" on the cock-sucking so that you can enjoy the subtle sensations that your other is providing. I've included it as the last lesson because of this. A lot of individuals believe that giving your lover the deep throat technique is the pinnacle of pleasure-giving. In fact, I think the number sixty-nine represents the pinnacle of pleasure. When executed correctly and selflessly, and when both of you are fully aware of one other's deepest wants, the sixty-nine is the best. However, most people practice it too early and it becomes an enjoyable experience for one partner at the expense of the other because of the issue that was discussed previously in this session. You will find that this is the most efficient way to give and receive pleasure when you are fully attuned to one another. The prerequisite is straightforward: the two of you have to be total cocksuckers! To attempt sixty-nine is to call for discontent in your relationship if your spouse is merely interested in receiving attention and has no interest in lending it. TECHNIQUES In my capacity as editor of FRENCH CUISINE MAGAZINE, I occasionally enquire more about our members by sending them questionnaires. I inquire about their preferences for safe and sensible oral sex practices and their desires. The following are some of the most well-liked cock-sucking techniques. THE BUTTERFLY FLUTTER: Kneeling over your spouse is the ideal position for this sensual cock-sucking motion.

Kneel between his knees if he is lying on his back. Alternately, as your spouse stands, kneel in front of him. This is my Favorite position because you can play with his balls with total freedom, and the cock feels thicker in your mouth and throat. I was first introduced to this method in northern California by a cocksucker. In the heart of San Francisco, there once stood a famed movie theatre with a darkened balcony—a refuge for cocksuckers. And we were all set for this man.

The moans coming from the guy's throat as his cock was being sucked told you that this was one of a thousand guys who knew how to satisfy a range of fresh cock-meat cravings. I observed him intently while he was sucking cock because it felt so amazing. I came down close to the cock and watched how he was navigating it in addition to watching the guys who were receiving the radical suck. He applied a primary suction pressure to the cock, but just enough to barely bring the shaft into his mouth. His lips tightly encircling the man's large, swollen cock, he would softly flick the tip of the cock with his tongue. He opened his mouth to contact the tip of the cock with the tip of his tongue, encircling it at a depth. He would move his tongue up and down around the cock shaft with his lips. His tongue would flick up and down the tip of his cock. It would help if you gave it a try. At any hour you like, it will force your Butterfly Flutter companion back into your mouth. After a few minutes, carry on with the fundamental vacuum suction.